Messy Bessey's
HOLIDAYS

by
Patricia
and
Fredrick
McKissack

illustrated
by Dana
Regan

Children's Press®
A Division of Scholastic Inc
New York • Toronto • London • Auckland • Sydney
Mexico City • New Delhi • Hong Kong
Danbury, Connecticut

To Roberta and Phil Duyff–thanks for the many holiday celebrations.
—P. and F. M.

To the Regans
—D. R.

Reading Consultant
Linda Cornwell
Learning Resource Consultant
Indiana Department of Education

Visit Children's Press® on the Internet at:
http://publishing.grolier.com

Library of Congress Cataloging-in-Publication Data
McKissack, Pat.
    Messy Bessey's holidays / by Patricia and Fredrick McKissack; illustrated by
Dana Regan.
        p. cm. — (Rookie reader)
    Summary: Bessey and her mother bake cookies for Christmas, Kwanzaa, and
Hanukkah, and after cleaning up the kitchen, they distribute the treats to their
neighbors.
    ISBN 0-516-20829-2 (lib. bdg.)   0-516-26476-1 (pbk.)
    [1. Baking—Fiction. 2. Cleanliness—Fiction. 3. Christmas—Fiction.
4. Kwanzaa—Fiction. 5. Hanukkah—Fiction. 6. Stories in rhyme.]
I. McKissack, Fredrick. II. Regan, Dana, ill. III. Title. IV. Series.
PZ8.3.M224Mds 1999
[E]—dc21   98-8057
                                                  CIP
                                                  AC

Recipe on page 31 adapted from Betty Crocker's New Cookbook, 1996. *Used with
permission of General Mills, Inc.*

11 12 13 14 15 R 08 07   62

December holidays are great—
a time for fun and cheer.

Christmas, Kwanzaa, Chanukah
and the coming New Year.

Bessey's in the kitchen
busy as can be
baking holiday cookies
for her friends and family.

Ummm!
Those cookies smell so good.
They're sure to taste good, too.

8

But Messy Bessey look around.
There is something you must do.

12

While working
you have made a mess.
Things are out of place.

Keep your kitchen safe and clean by wiping up your space.

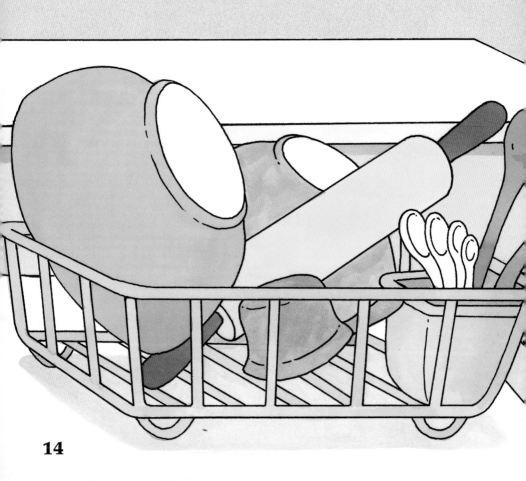

Wonderful job, Miss Bessey!
The kitchen looks just great.

17

Your cookies tell a story
of how we celebrate.

Eight menorah candles
lit each and every night
of the Jewish Chanukah holiday,
a festival of light.

20

21

These are happy angels
who sang on Christmas morn
to shepherds on a hillside
that Jesus Christ was born.

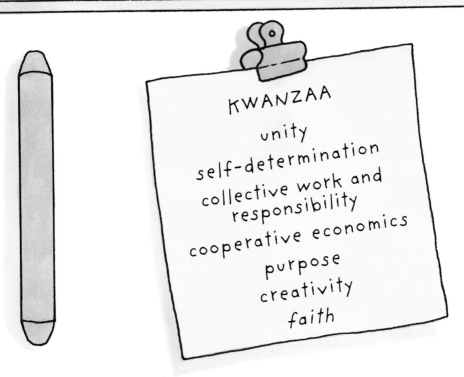

KWANZAA

unity
self-determination
collective work and
responsibility
cooperative economics
purpose
creativity
faith

African-Americans' Kwanzaa
is a week of community sharing.
Families gather to feast and learn
through the seven ways of caring.

25

Menorahs, candles, fruits, and bells
are signs of the holidays.

All over, people celebrate

in many different ways.

Christmas,
Kwanzaa,
and Chanukah,
no matter what the reason,
here's a gift from Bess to you
to celebrate the season.

DECORATED SUGAR COOKIES

*Ask an adult to help you make
these delicious holiday treats!*

1 1/2 cups powdered sugar
1 cup margarine or butter, softened
1 tsp. vanilla
1/2 tsp. almond extract
1 large egg
2 1/2 cups all-purpose flour
1 tsp. baking soda
1 tsp. cream of tartar

1. Mix powdered sugar, margarine, vanilla, almond extract, and egg in large bowl. Stir in remaining ingredients. Cover and refrigerate at least 2 hours.

2. Heat oven to 375°. Grease cookie sheet lightly with shortening.

3. Divide dough in half. Roll each half 1/4-inch thick on lightly floured surface. Cut into desired shapes with 2- to 2 1/2-inch cookie cutters. Place on cookie sheet.

4. Bake 7 to 8 minutes or until edges are light brown. Remove from cookie sheet. Cool on wire rack.

5. Frost and decorate cooled cookies with frosting, tinted with food coloring. Decorate with colored sugar, small candies, fruit, or nuts if desired.

Makes about 5 dozen 2-inch cookies.

Word List (132 words)

a	Chanukah	gather	lit	safe	time
African-	cheer	gift	look	sang	to
Americans	Christ	good	looks	season	too
all	Christmas	great	made	seven	ummm
and	clean	happy	many	sharing	up
angels	coming	have	matter	shepherds	was
are	community	her	menorah	signs	ways
around	cookies	here's	menorahs	smell	we
as	December	hillside	mess	so	week
baking	different	holiday	messy	something	what
be	do	holidays	Miss	space	while
bells	each	how	morn	story	who
Bess	eight	in	must	sure	wiping
Bessey	every	is	new	taste	wonderful
Bessey's	families	Jesus	night	tell	working
born	family	Jewish	no	that	year
busy	feast	job	of	the	you
but	festival	just	on	there	your
by	for	keep	out	these	
can	friends	kitchen	over	they're	
candles	from	Kwanzaa	people	Things	
caring	fruits	learn	place	those	
celebrate	fun	light	reason	through	

About the Authors

Patricia and Fredrick McKissack are award-winning authors living in Missouri. They are the recipients of the Coretta Scott King Award, the Jane Addams Peace Award, the Newbery Honor, and the 1998 Regina Medal from the Catholic Library Association. The McKissacks have written every *Messy Bessey* book in the Rookie Reader® series.

About the Illustrator

Dana Regan was born and raised in northern Wisconsin. She now lives in Missouri with her husband, Dan, and her sons, Joe and Tommy.